D0892104

First Facts®

FACT FILES

AMERICAN SYMBOLS

What You Need to Know

by MELISSA FERGUSON

CAPSTONE PRESS
a capstone imprint

First Facts are published by Capstone Press,
1710 Roe Crest Drive, North Mankato, Minnesota 56003
www.mycapstone.com

Library of Congress Cataloging-in-Publication Data
Library of Congress Cataloging-in-Publication data is available on the Library of Congress website.
ISBN 978-1-5157-8116-5 (library binding)
ISBN 978-1-5157-8127-1 (paperback)
ISBN 978-1-5157-8133-2 (eBook PDF)

Editorial Credits

Mandy Robbins, editor; Jenny Bergstrom, designer; Kelly Garvin, media researcher; Laura Manthe, production specialist

Photo Credits

Flags of the World/Rick Wyatt, 7, (bottom middle); Library of Congress Prints and Photographs Division, 4; Newscom/Staff KRT, 17; Shutterstock: Allen.G, 3, amadeustx, 24, Andrea Izzotti, 21, Aperature51, 18, bikeriderlondon, 5, Bildagentur Zoonar GmbH, 9, blurAZ, 13, Bruce Stansfield, 7 (top middle), charnsitr, 7 (bottom), Cory A. Ulrich, 7 (left), cosma, 12, Dean Fikar, cover (top right), DenisFilm, 22, Edwin Verin, backcover, Everett Historical, 11, 16, 17 (insets), gary718, cover (top left), Jannarong, 10, Marco Rubino, 14, Matej Hudovernik, 19 (left), Neil Phillip Mey, 7 (top), Orhan Cam, cover (bottom right), UbjsP, cover (bottom left), 1, Songquan Deng, 15, T photography, 19 (right), Tory Kallman, 8

Printed in China.
010295F17

Table of Contents

America's Famous Symbols

The United States has many symbols. They are part of the country's history. A symbol is something that stands for something else. For example, a heart is a symbol of love. You may have heard the "Star-Spangled Banner" at sports events. This song is a symbol of American **patriotism**.

patriotism—showing love and loyalty to one's country

The American Flag

The American flag is a symbol of the United States. The flag's nickname is "Old Glory." Its colors are red, white, and blue. White stands for purity. Red means strength. Blue stands for justice.

The flag has 50 stars. There is one star for each state in the nation. The flag's 13 stripes stand for the 13 original **colonies**.

FACT

Astronauts Neil Armstrong and Edwin "Buzz" Aldrin put an American flag on the moon in 1969.

colonies—the 13 British territories that became the United States of America

THE AMERICAN FLAG

THROUGH THE YEARS

1776
Unofficial

1820-1830
Bennington Flag

1877
38 Star Flag

PRESENT
Flag with 50 stars

The Bald Eagle

The bald eagle has been a symbol of the United States since 1782. It represents strength and bravery.

Bald eagles make their homes in North America. They almost went ***extinct*** by 1963. There are now laws that protect them.

FACT

Benjamin Franklin thought the turkey was a more respectable choice for the national bird. He said bald eagles only stole food from other animals.

extinct—no longer living; an extinct animal is one that has died out, with no more of its kind

Uncle Sam

Uncle Sam is a symbol of the United States government. The image of Uncle Sam first appeared in drawings and books around 1812.

In the early 1900s, the government needed men to join the army during World War I (1914–1918). Uncle Sam's image encouraged people to support their country.

ARTIST
James Montgomery Flagg

MODEL
Flagg used his own face as a model

I WANT YOU FOR U.S. ARMY

NEAREST RECRUITING STATION

MORE THAN 4 MILLION COPIES were printed between 1917 and 1918 while the U.S. was involved in World War I.

THE REAL UNCLE SAM

Was there a real Uncle Sam? Legend has it his name was Sam Wilson. He was a New York meat-packer in the early 1800s. Wilson sent barrels of meat to U.S. soldiers fighting in the War of 1812. He stamped the letters "U.S." on the barrels. From this, soldiers nicknamed him Uncle Sam. His nickname eventually became connected to the U.S. government.

The Great Seal

The Great Seal is a symbol of **independence**. This **emblem** is used on important government papers. It can also be found on the $1 bill.

independence—freedom from the control of other people or things
emblem—a symbol or a sign

WHAT THE
GREAT SEAL
MEANS

E PLURIBUS UNUM

This phrase is Latin for "Out of Many, One." It represents how Americans are united.

CLOUD OF STARS

The cloud of stars represents a new nation taking its place among other nations.

BALD EAGLE

The bald eagle is the national bird of the United States. It stands for courage and strength.

THE NUMBER 13

The number 13 is seen often on the Great Seal. It stands for the 13 original states. There are 13 arrows, 13 stripes in the shield, and 13 stars.

OLIVE BRANCH

The olive branch is a symbol of peace.

ARROWS

Arrows show a readiness for battle.

SHIELD

The shield stands for the nation standing strong in the world.

The Liberty Bell

The Liberty Bell is a symbol of freedom. It was made in 1752 for the Pennsylvania State House. Today that building is called Independence Hall. The words on the bell tell Americans to spread freedom to all people throughout the land.

FACT

The Liberty Bell is on the $100 bill that was designed in 2009.

The Liberty Bell has a crack in its side.
It was last rung on George Washington's
birthday in 1846.

Ellis Island

Twelve million **immigrants** entered the United States between 1892 and 1954. Many left hard times for a fresh start.

New York City's Ellis Island was the first stop for many immigrants. Workers there asked immigrants questions about themselves. They ruled out any criminals. Doctors made sure immigrants were healthy. Those who passed **inspection** were allowed into America.

immigrant—a person who leaves one country and settles in another
inspection—the process of looking over or reviewing something

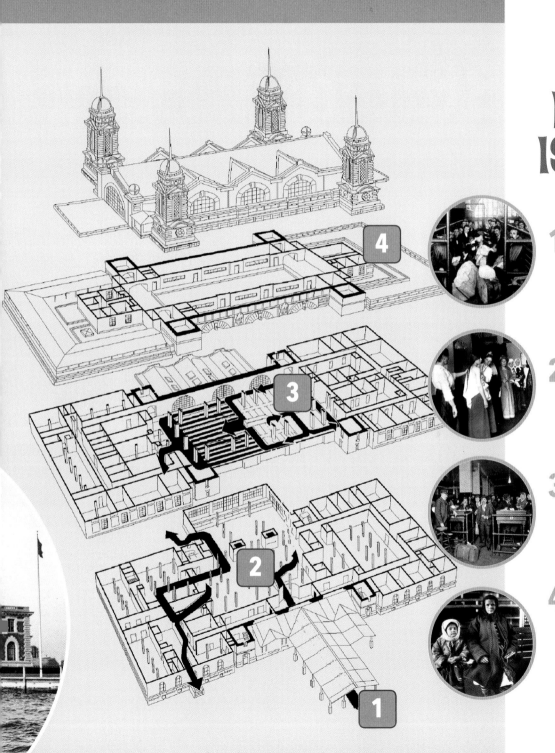

MOVING THROUGH
ELLIS ISLAND

1 **THE REGISTRY ROOM**

Immigrants waited to be inspected.

2 **MEDICAL EXAM**

Sick people were held back.

3 **LEGAL INSPECTION**

Immigrants were asked 29 questions.

4 **THE KISSING POST**

Immigrants who passed inspection reunited with loved ones.

The Statue of Liberty

The Statue of Liberty stands in New York **Harbor**. It was a gift to America from France in 1886. "Lady Liberty" is a sign of friendship between the countries. It also represents freedom and hope.

FACT

The Statue of Liberty started out the color of a copper penny. It has turned green from being outside so long.

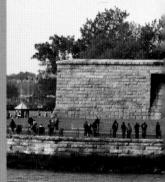

harbor—a place where ships load and unload passengers and cargo

The statue was the first American symbol many immigrants saw upon entering the United States. Immigrants still come to America hoping for better lives.

The White House

The White House is a symbol of **democracy**. It represents the United States' history. U.S. presidents have lived and worked in the White House since 1800.

democracy—a form of government in which the citizens vote for their leaders

Have you heard of the Oval Office?
It's where the president does a lot of
important business. The Oval Office is
in the White House.

Glossary

colonies (KAH-luh-nees)—the 13 British territories that became the United States of America

democracy (di-MAH-kruh-see)—a form of government in which the citizens vote for their leaders

emblem (EM-bluhm)—a symbol or a sign

extinct (ik-STINGKT)—no longer living; an extinct animal is one that has died out, with no more of its kind

harbor (HAR-bur)—a place where ships load and unload passengers and cargo

immigrant (IM-uh-gruhnt)—a person who leaves one country and settles in another

independence (in-di-PEN-duhnss)—freedom from the control of other people or things

inspection (in-SPEK-shuhn)—the process of looking over or reviewing something

patriotism (PAY-tree-uh-tiz-uhm)—showing love and loyalty to one's country

Read More

Alderman, Peter. *The Rocket's Red Glare: Celebrating the History of The Star Spangled Banner.* Toronto: Flowerpot Children's Press, Inc., 2014.

Malam, John. *You Wouldn't Want to Be a Worker on the Statue of Liberty!: A Monument You'd Rather Not Build.* New York: Franklin Watts, an imprint of Scholastic Inc., 2017.

Monroe, Tyler. *The American Flag.* U.S. Symbols. Mankato, Minn.: Capstone Press, 2013.

Internet Sites

Use FactHound find Internet sites related to this book.

1. Visit *www.facthound.com*

2. Just type in 9781515781165

Check out projects, games and lots more at
www.capstonekids.com

Critical Thinking Questions

1. What do the colors in the American Flag stand for?

2. Which symbol discussed in this book do you think best represents the United States of America? Why?

3. Why do you think that the Statue of Liberty was put up in New York Harbor?

Index